C.L. BAIRD

INSPIRATIONAL LEADER

The Ultimate Guide on How to Be an Exceptional Leader, Learn the Different Effective Ways You Can Truly Inspire Your Team and Watch Extraordinary Things Happen

Descrierea CIP a Bibliotecii Naţionale a României
C.L. BAIRD
    INSPIRATIONAL LEADER. The Ultimate Guide on How to Be an Exceptional Leader, Learn the Different Effective Ways You Can Truly Inspire Your Team and Watch Extraordinary Things Happen / C.L. Baird. – Bucharest: Editura My Ebook, 2020
    ISBN

C.L. BAIRD

INSPIRATIONAL LEADER

**The Ultimate Guide on How to Be an Exceptional Leader, Learn
the Different Effective Ways You Can Truly Inspire Your Team
and Watch Extraordinary Things Happen**

My Ebook Publishing House
Bucharest, 2020

TABLE OF CONTENTS

INTRODUCTION

Most of us will never have seen ourselves as being leaders. For the majority of us, the thought of taking charge of an office will not so long ago have seemed completely absurd. That's a job for high fliers, for people-people... for born leaders!

But despite any initial apprehension, leadership roles are something that many of us will have thrust upon us against any protestations. In the vast majority of industries, progress and a hike in salary *means* taking on more responsibility. And that responsibility will very often take the form of some kind of leadership role. You can only progress so far before you start having staff under you and the further you then climb the ladder, the more people will start looking to you for direction and the more people you'll be responsible for.

That then leaves two choices: shy away from the pressure and the responsibility and live on the modest salary that comes from that, or learn to suck it up and take charge.

And guess what? When you do accept that mantle and become the leader that you can be, you'll find that it's one of the best experiences imaginable for your personal growth and development. You'll become more confident, more able and more authoritative and it can completely transform the way you see yourself.

So now the big question: can you *learn* leadership? Are some people simply destined to be good leaders while others will forever be disrespected and awkward in the role?

Well, while some people are 'born with it' (as Maybeline would have us believe), it certainly *is* possible to learn the skills needed for leadership if you don't already have them. And as it happens, that's exactly what this book is about to do for you!

So read on and prepare to learn the ins and outs of leadership and what it takes to inspire a team and get the very most out of them.

What you will learn...

- What makes a great leader
- Should you be feared or liked?
- How to become instantly more charismatic

- How to use ancient techniques like 'transformismo' to control your team
- How to understand the differences of your team and get them to work for you
- How to handle a crisis
- How to cultivate inspiration
- How to give your staff motivation How to create new teams

And more!

And once you've honed these skills, you'll find that they become powerful not *only* in the office and the boardroom but also in all other walks of life. Prepare to become a more inspiring friend and a more effective parent!

CHAPTER 1

WHAT MAKES A GREAT LEADER?

Perhaps the best place to start is by asking what makes a great leader. What is the end goal here? What are you aspiring to?

When we think of great leaders, we will often think of inspiring superhero types. People with heroic, puffed out chests, powerful voices and a cool air of confidence. They always know the right thing to do and they have the uncanny ability to reel off motivational and inspiration speeches at the drop of a hat. No one ever defies these great leaders because they don't want to – the leaders are so just and wise that they have no need. But if anyone ever *did* cross them, they would be immediately be put to rights with a stern but fair judgement and unquestionable authority. These are the leaders that make us feel safe, that steer our ships through uncharted waters and that make us feel like we can do anything as a team. These are the heroes taken straight out of the Saturday morning cartoons you probably watched as a child (which, by the way, are based very much on our Father and Mother archetypes).

Now the chances are that you probably have known a few people like this in your lifetime. Perhaps you have a parent who really is that wise, all-knowing figure. Or maybe you had a teacher that inspired you when you were younger and helped you to make the career choices that led you to where you are today.

You might also know of some famous real-life characters who fit this bill. Perhaps you know of a few celebrities who you look up to, or a few historical characters even.

But for the most part, this is not the reality of what makes a good leader. While all these things could certainly help you to inspire followers, they are certainly not necessary for you to become an effective leader. And it's just as well - as that would be an awful lot of pressure to put on yourself!

So what does make a good leader? What is the minimum entry requirement?

Of course this is a somewhat abstract concept and not one that can be satisfied with a simple answer. But let's give it the best shot.

Ultimately, the best leader is the leader who gets results. And they do this by organizing, stabilizing and motivating a team in order to get more out of them than they would be able to accomplish on their own. So put simply: does having this leader in place make a big difference to the team's ability to accomplish goals?

If the answer is yes, then the leader is providing a useful function and they are worth keeping in place. If the answer is no, then you could make the argument that the leader is not useful and is a waste of money or time.

But this mentality, while accurate, is dangerous. Why? Because it leads to 'performance reviews' and other tests to identify the ability of the leader. A leader might then be punished or penalized if they should fail to meet monthly targets, or if they should be seen to be spending too much money. This seems to make sense when you think about leaders in terms of their ability to help teams meet goals but this is forgetting one small factor: time.

Because a leader's ability should not be measured in terms of their ability to accomplish X in T amount of time. If that is the only concern and the only aspect of performance that the leader is graded on, then in all likelihood they will end up making the wrong decisions for the good of the business and the

13

good of the team. They will stick with what works, they will stick with what they know and they will avoid taking risks or evolving their business model to meet new challenges. A good leader should be someone who is able to see the road ahead and to seemingly pre-empt the changes that will affect businesses most.

These are the leaders who will be able to help a business to grow rather than just survive and who will be able to help avoid catastrophic failures that lead to layoffs or bankruptcy. And this same theory applies in other contexts too - the best parent is one who can not only keep the family happy and functioning well but who can also help to improve their circumstances so that they become happier and so that they become more fulfilled. They are also able to foresee potential challenges and set up contingencies so that they can deal with crises while remaining cool and level headed. This is the true example of 'Super Dad' and 'Super Mum'.

So we can conclude that a great leader is able to help a team meet goals more effectively than they would otherwise and that these goals should be long term goals rather than short term. When a leader is stifled, it is very often because the leader above them is short sighted. If management higher up is forcing quarterly reviews with strict, punitive measures for those seen to

14

be under performing then it will stifle a leader's ability to grow and bring changes. This means that the goal needs to be right as well and in many ways, it's that goal that we will see is the most important driving force behind a great leader.

Traits of a Great Leader

That's a rather abstract overview of leadership though and one that doesn't really give us all that much concrete information to work with. So let's take a look at some of the more concrete traits that we can break down this concept into…

What is a good leader?

Good leaders believe in what they're doing

Perhaps one of the single most important things for a good leader is that they believe in what they are doing. That is to say that good leaders should have a real passion for what they're doing and really believe in it. This is important because it will help them to make the best decisions for the long term of the business and also because it will help them to inspire others.

Good leaders see the big picture

A good leader needs to be able to step back and see the bigger picture. They need to understand where the team is headed and what challenges will face them along the way. This is important because it will allow all the individual members of that team to focus on their smaller aspect.

Good leaders have broad knowledge

A good leader should be something of a jack of all trades. The reason for this, is that it will give them the understanding to see how all the pieces fit together and it will mean they are able to deal with issues as they arise across departments; even when that means taking more of a top-level approach rather than understanding the nitty gritty.

You'll also find that having some basic experience in each aspect of your business can help you to get more respect from the professionals in each aspect of your organization.

Good leaders understand people

A good leader should be able to work with anyone. This means they need to be able to empathize with those people and to understand what makes them tick so that they can inspire them to take action. It also means that a good leader needs to know how to

Good leaders are great communicators

This also means you need to be able to communicate as a leader. Not only is it your job to communicate the plan in a way that your team can fully understand but it is also your job to communicate to your superiors and to your clientele.

Good leaders think ahead

A good leader shouldn't just be dealing with the day-to-day challenges of the business, but should be thinking one step ahead. You need to be constantly questioning what the next challenge will be and how to face it and you need to be thinking about how to grow, improve and scale your organization.

Good leaders have contingency plans

Good leaders also need to have multiple contingencies and backup plans. Think of your worst case scenarios and be prepared for them.

Good leaders lead by example

It is important that you lead by example in all cases. This means that you need to take a 'do as I do' approach, rather than making one rule for one person and another for yourself.

It also means more generally setting the tone. Teams look to their leaders as barometers – to identify how serious any given situation is and to know how they should react. If you panic, then your team will panic. If you stay calm, then your team will too.

Good leaders are courageous

A good leader needs to be courageous. If this is sounding like your Saturday morning TV show again, then bear in mind that we're not talking about the kind of courage that gives you the strength to stand up to the Decepticons in Transformers. Rather, we're talking about the courage to take risks and to break the mold. This is very important

Good leaders take responsibility

Once you have made that decision, it is critical that you stand by it and face the music. That means that you need to accept responsibility when things go wrong. This can seem unfair at times but once again, it is actually a feature that is important for the welfare of the team. By accepting responsibility, you remove culpability from your team and give them the freedom to work without fear of repercussions.

CHAPTER 2

HOW TO INSPIRE YOUR TEAM

Now you have a broad idea of what it means to be a good leader, it's time to break this down and to examine each of these points in more detail.

But the most important point we can discuss is inspiration. If you can inspire your team to work, then you can get the very best out of them no matter what else. If they believe in your vision, they will be absolutely loyal and absolutely committed to what you're doing. They will work harder and longer hours and they will drive your business, department or startup forward faster than anyone else.

Notice the word 'vision' here. That's very important and we'll come to why in a moment.

What's more, is that if you have a vision for your team, you'll help to inspire *others*. That means your customers and your potential business partners. More people will want to work with you. More people will want to buy from you. And more people will want to be loyal to your brand and to think of themselves as a 'part' of what you do.

It goes deeper too. That's because having a vision can also help you to make the right decisions for your organization. We talked briefly about the importance of not just keeping your team afloat but of growing and avoiding catastrophe? That all comes from having the right vision.

Your vision is what gives you your goal. And if you get it right, it should also be what gives you your drive to succeed and makes that passion contagious. Many of the points we talk about later in this book will stem from that vision.

Introducing: The Golden Circle

Perhaps the best way to illustrate what is meant by this, is to look at a concept in business known as the 'golden circle'. What is the golden circle?

Well, if you believe the highly popular TED talk by Simon Sinek (who first proposed the concept), the golden circle is the difference between innovating companies that grow and thrive and those companies that fail.

Why is it that Apple is constantly creating more exciting products he asks? (This was a while ago, bear in mind...).

Why is it that the Wright Brothers' succeeded where others failed, others who had more resources and more means?

The answer is the golden circle.

The golden circle is made of three 'rings' which can be seen like layers. On the outermost ring, you have the word 'What'. Inside that, you have the word 'How'. And on the innermost ring, is the word 'Why'.

So as a leader, you need to think about these three things:

- What?

- How?

- Why?

For the sake of simplicity, we will start by focusing on this question from a business perspective. That means we can change these questions into:

- What do you do?

- How do you do it?

- Why do you do it?

And the key aspect to all this is that last part – the *why*. The most important question you can possibly ask yourself as a business is *why* you do what you do.

And what might surprise you is that a lot of people can't answer this question. What they tell you is that they are in their business to make money. Other than that, what 'why' is there?

This is where your company 'mission statement' comes in and this is something that all the most successful businesses in the world have in common – great mission statements. It is the company with the mission statement that actually believes in something, that has a strong brand and that other people can get behind.

Some examples:

Ikea

At IKEA, our vision is to create a better everyday life for the many people. Our business idea supports this vision by offering a wide range of well - designed functional home furnishing products at prices so low that as many people as possible will be able to afford them.

Amazon

It is our goal to be Earth's most customer-centric company, where customers can find and discover anything they might want to buy online.

Coca-Cola

To refresh the world in mind, body and spirit. To inspire moments of optimism and happiness through our brands and actions. To create value and make a difference.

Facebook

Facebook's mission is to give people the power to share make the world a more open and connected.

Google

Google's mission is to organize the world's information and make it universally accessible and useful.

Intel

Delight our customers, employees and shareholders by relentlessly delivering the platform and technology advancements that become essential to the way we work and live.

McDonald's

McDonald's brand mission is to be our customers' favorite place and way to eat and drink.

Microsoft

Our mission is to enable people and businesses throughout the world to realize their full potential.

This is important because it is what makes the brand something that the audience, the employees and the leaders themselves can believe in – and it is what sets the long-term course for the journey.

And as Simon Sinek puts it: people don't buy what you do, people buy *why you do it*.

The objective is not to sell to people who need what you make, the objective is to sell to people who believe in what you believe. Those are the people who will be loyal to your brand.

And the same goes for employees. Employees who believe in your mission statement will stay up late at night working because they believe in what they do – they're excited by it and they want to see it happen.

Heck, people on Kickstarter will even pay to see your mission statement become a reality even when there's nothing in it for them. Oculus' mission statement is to: deliver incredible, affordable and ubiquitous consumer virtual reality to the world. This is a mission that people believed in so strongly, that they essentially funded the organization and allowed it to become a real-life company.

A good business starts with that vision and then builds outward from there – everything from the branding, to the marketing, to the products themselves should align with that eventual endgoal.

And when you're excited about your goals, it will be infectious. When you're excited about where your business is going, it will come across in the way you gesticulate, the way you talk and the way you lead. And this is what will make people follow you to the ends of the Earth.

Finding Your Vision

Start-ups are often described as being in a 'state of flow'. What does this mean?

Well, according to *The Rise of Superman*, written by Steven Kotler, a 'flow state' is a state where we are incredibly highly focused, creative and resourceful. At this point, our prefrontal cortices shut down (resulting in a state called 'temporo-hypofrontality'). This is because we are so engaged with what we are doing, that we actually completely lose track of everything else – it's like when you come out of a cinema and feel as though you've been in a dream.

Startups are described as being in a constant state of flow because they are so passionate and so driven that they lose their subjective reality and are 100% engaged with their mission and goal.

If you create a business, then you should start from the ground up. Think about not only the bottom line but also the way you're going to achieve and why you were passionate to get into this industry in the first place. Do you love green food and want to make the world a greener place? Do you just love business and want to empower other organizations to do more? Do you believe that happiness comes from being well dressed and confident in your skin? Do you live and breathe fitness and want others to feel the same?

Find your passion and then build your business around that ideal from the ground up.

But what if you inherit your business or your industry and you have no say in the matter? If you've just been elevated to 'area manager' then you might not have been involved in choosing the organization's direction of vision.

And what if you have already created your business and it's too late to 'start' with your vision?

Well, in the latter scenario you need to take a step back and re-assess your organization. There probably *is* a strong 'why' behind what you do, even if you can't see what that is yet. You were probably drawn to your current niche and business model for a reason – so what is that. What are you doing differently from the competition? If you had limitless resources, what would you do with them?

Another strategy you can try is to ask yourself the 'five whys'. This is a technique that we can use to get to the bottom of why we do something. And it's simple: you ask yourself 'why' five times.

- *Why did you make a fitness site?*
- Because I love fitness.
- *Why?*
- Because being fit makes me feel healthy and capable.
- *Why is that important?*
- Because then I can do anything.

- *Why is that important?*

- Because then I feel free.

- *Why is that important?*

- Because freedom is what makes me feel happy.

So essentially, you can then retroactively shape your business around this core value: freedom and happiness. Perhaps your logo becomes someone running through the grass and maybe you create an Instagram account filled with people taking full advantage of their bodies to express that freedom.

Now what about that second scenario? What about when you 'inherit' the business? How do you find the 'why' then?

One method is to ask the business owner – or *your* leader – what it is that drives them. If you can get behind their vision and make it your own, then you might stand a good chance of inspiring your team and your customers. If you can't and if you don't believe in what the company is doing… then the chances are that you won't be the best leader you could be and that this organization isn't for you.

The best thing you can do to make the very most of your abilities and to ensure you are contributing all that you can… is to leave that organization and look elsewhere.

This might be extreme, but think of the leaders you've known who are the least effective. What is it about them that makes them so? Chances are you'll have noticed they always have a demeanor of disinterest and lack of enthusiasm. And this is there undoing.

Don't be that person – find an organization you really believe in. Or build one!

Oh and for family life, or your personal life, you can have visions too. A vision is just like a goal in this context except that you are going to visualize it and think about the way it *feels* more than just the metrics. Instead of thinking you'd like your family to 'be richer', this might mean imagining your family living in a bigger house, without stress and with all the things you'd like.

This is important because having a vision rather than a goal means you can be more flexible about how you get there – and take the best route to get the results you want. It will also keep you *much* more motivated, which actually comes down to the very structure of your brain!

CHAPTER 3

HOW TO INCENTIVIZE THE RIGHT WAY

So you're passionate about what you do now and that comes across in the way you talk and the decisions you make. The next challenge is how you're going to pass this on to your staff and your team so that they feel the same way.

And you can't expect them to be *as* passionate about everything as you to begin with. Sure, it would be nice if they were and if they had that 'implicit' motivation. But in reality, a lot of your staff are just there to make money so that they can go home to their partners and kids. They have their own dreams.

So how do you motivate them and get them on board?

Why Incentives Don't Work

One method is to try and use incentives: that means offering money or other rewards. Unfortunately though, this simply doesn't tend to work – it fosters poor teamwork and can actually prevent your team from working their best.

It can even make a team *less* motivated!

This is best illustrated by something called the 'candle experiment', which is an experiment designed to test creativity. Specifically, it is designed to test the ability to overcome a 'cognitive bias' called 'functional fixedness'.

Essentially, functional fixedness causes us to get stuck in one way of thinking, usually about a tool or a task. Here, we tend to fixate on one way of doing something, to the point where we can no longer think of any other solutions or any other contexts.

So for example, if someone were to give you a hammer and ask you to open a window, you might smash the glass rather than use the hammer as a lever to pry the window open. Why? Because you can only think of the hammer terms of its main use: hitting things. It requires an extra level of creativity to think outside of that box and to look at a hammer as an implement that can be used in any of a wide number of different ways.

To test this ability, the candle experiment presents participants with a box of tacks and a candle and then asks them to attach the candle to the wall so that it can burn. Most people will attempt to tack the candle to the wall and will find it continually falls off.

But the solution is in fact to tack the *box* to the wall and then to stand the candle inside it. This requires participants to think outside that box and to think of the box as a part of the experiment and a resource. One way you can do this is by using the psychological experiment of breaking down all the items you have into their constituent parts and materials: you don't have a candle, you have a candle, wax and string for example. A box of tacks is tacks, a box, cardboard and metal.

What's interesting and relevant about this study is that when an incentive is introduced (a reward for the person who first comes up with the solution), performance actually goes down. This makes sense from a neuroscience perspective because motivation gives us focus and focus makes it hard for us to see all possibilities.

Flow states on the other hand encourage the brain to produce anandamide – a neurotransmitter that is correlated with creativity and lateral thinking. So you need to move your team *away* from working toward a reward and *toward* thinking of the work as rewarding in itself.

Plus, we all know that as soon as we start doing something for money or for grades it becomes less fun. This is why no one enjoys their college courses – even though they chose the subject!

Teamwork and Incentives

The other problem with incentives is that they actually make us less likely to work as teams. One way to think about this is by looking at the military.

In the military, one member will often be willing to *give their life* for the rest of the team. And they are rewarded for this mentality – they are rewarded for sacrificing their own needs for the betterment of everyone else.

But in the case of business, we are often encouraged instead to sacrifice others in order to get ahead. We are rewarded for making the most sales in our team, which encourages us to pilfer sales from other salesmen and women.

Rewarding individuals gives them a good reason to tread on each other to get ahead.

Ownership, Autonomy and Understanding

So if you can't just pay your staff to work harder, what *can* you do? The answer is to give them ownership, autonomy and understanding. In other words, you:

- Let them take credit for what they do and put their name omit

- You give them the freedom to do things their own way

- And you give them the understanding so they know *why* they're doing it

This first part is important because it gives your staff a certain amount of pride in what they're doing. If your team feel as though they are working on their own projects and as though they will get rewarded for the work they do, then they have a very good reason to work harder. Again, in this case the work becomes its *ownreward*.

Give someone a 'project' and let them put their stamp on it and they can use this as a way to prove their skills, something to add to their CVs and a challenge. Let someone create their own sections on your website with their name on it and it becomes something they will be proud of and that they can show their friends and family – they *will* work harder on it!

And finally, you need to make sure your team understand the 'why'. This is important because it allows you to stop micromanaging and to give your team agency over the way they do their products. That and we've already seen how motivating a simple 'why' can be.

So instead of telling someone to 'move those boxes from A to B using the forklift and in no less than 2 hours', tell them 'the pickup truck is coming tomorrow to collect the inventory, make sure it's ready'. This not only gives them the ability to work their way, to be smart about it and potentially get time off and to get the sense of reward that comes from solving problems; it *also* allows them to make critical decisions without referring to you for help every time there's a stumbling block.

Imagine giving those first set of instructions and then the forklift breaks down. In this scenario, your team may now not know what to do! They were told to use the forklift so all they can do is to come and ask you what plan B is.

But with the second set of instructions they were never explicitly told to use the forklift so they might instead decide to get the team to chip in and lift the palettes. Or they might find a way to get the pickup truck further into the warehouse. It's up to them – and this is when people do their best work *and* you can stay less involved.

But remember, you still need to take responsibility for their decisions. This is the mark of a good leader and it is what will give your team the confidence to make those kinds of choices.

CHAPTER 4

HOW TO INCREASE
YOUR CHARISMA AND AUTHORITY

This is all well and good but you will still benefit greatly from simply being able to deliver a moving speech, or being able to communicate what people need to do.

Communication is particularly important because it is what will prevent avoidable mistakes. If you are not able to communicate what needs to be done or why, then people will set about completing the wrong task and with the best will in the world, there will be mistakes.

Likewise, charisma and charm will instantly help to convey the passion you have and to get people on board. Your aim is to become a better orator and to better communicate the vision you have for your team and the reasons why it matters.

So how do you go about doing this?

How to Deliver a Great Speech

The first thing to do is to go back and read chapters 1 thru 3. Vision and passion once again come in up top here because they are what will help you to come across as someone who truly believes in what you're saying.

As soon as you really believe in what you're saying, this will come across in the way you do everything. It will show in your expression, it will show in the content of what you are saying and it will show in the way you move about up front and gesticulate.

Those gesticulations are important too. This is the way that you move your hands and your body as you speak and when you do it right, it can make a massive difference to how charming and convincing you seem. The most charismatic people in the world *all* get this right. When you can move your hands around and use big body language, you take up more space which makes people more interested and engaged with what you're saying. But you *also* demonstrate more conviction and congruence. This is the opposite of coming across like the shrinking wallflower who is perhaps embarrassed or shy of what they're saying.

The next thing you can do to demonstrate more confidence in what you're saying? Slow down! Showing confidence is very important because as mentioned – you are a barometer for the mood of your team. If you panic, then so too will everyone else. If you look confident, then people will have faith in what you're saying because *you* have that faith.

Slowing down will instantly help you to come across as more confident because we naturally speak quicker when we're nervous. What's more, is that slowing down will make what you're saying easier to follow, it will give you time to think of your next statement and it will make you appear objectively more intelligent. It even makes your voice sound deeper and helps it to project better.

There's something else subtle that is going on here too and that's that speaking too quickly can make you appear like you're trying to get everything out quickly because you're not sure people are going to want to listen for long. If you speak very fast, it might seem as though you're trying to get it all out before you get cut off. This is especially evident when it comes to telling stories: someone very confident who is a natural story teller will start by gradually setting the scene and creating context for their story. They will pause for dramatic effect and they will build up to the big reveals and punch lines. Think back

to the people who have held court at parties you've been to –
they all will have used this effect.

Or instead, try watching the videos of YouTuber Elliot
Hulse. He will often start with some kind of question or
statement and then leave a deliberate pause – with a gaze that
appears to look through the camera before following that
statement up. This is powerful stuff and you'll find that slowing
down like this and introducing silences is nerve wracking at
first. That's exactly *why* it takes confidence and precisely *how* it
will make you appear more confident if you start employing it as
a technique.

Effective Communication

Next up comes communication. This is something a lot of
people get wrong but it is definitely one of the most important
keys to success in almost every area of life.

So what *is* good communication?

The answer is that good communication is the ability to
convey precise meaning efficiently. Notice that work:
efficiently.

Your objective is to convey the exact meaning you want to
in the shortest amount of time. This keeps your 'communication

overhead' lower, so that less time is wasted on meetings and it will also help you to communicate what you need to communicate more efficiently with less margin for error.

This is why it's a big mistake to use too many big words or too much jargon. Often people do this to try and sound clever when in reality, it just makes them sound insecure – as though they have something to prove. What's more, is that it makes it harder for some people to understand and wastes people's time in reading.

So why *don't* you just use the fewest words possible and avoid those dramatic pauses entirely? If the only aim is efficiency, then why don't we all talk like robots?

This is where 'precision' comes into the equation. Precision is the ability to convey the *exact* meaning you want and often this means selecting the right word for the job. Saying 'it's cold today' has a subtly different meaning than saying 'it's freezing today'. What's more, is that the latter conveys more emotion at the same time – and it's that emotion that helps you to motivate and to make people take action (such as putting on a coat!). Seeing as the word 'freezing' actually conveys more information in fewer words, we can safely conclude that this word is actually more 'efficient' and thereby the slightly more decorative language in this case was the right choice.

When it comes to the written word, efficiency and accuracy become even more important. Make sure you learn your grammar and punctuation because a comma in the wrong place can equate to thousands of dollars lost!

The Law of Attraction

Another important tip to ensure you come across as more capable and more effective, is to make sure you *look* the part as well. This might seem shallow but the fact is that people are more inclined to follow others if they look like leaders.

That means you should take care in your presentation – in the way you dress, the way your hair looks and even your physical fitness. This makes you appear more capable altogether and it also makes it look like you *care* more. And we've already seen in detail why caring is so important when it comes to motivating a team.

This all boils down to what is known as the 'law of attraction'. If you look a certain way and act a certain way, then you will *become* the person you are already acting like. This is because you will change the way you feel about yourself and you will change the way others see you, therefore changing the way that others treat and respond to you.

As the saying goes: dress for the job you want!

Quick Exercise: How to Become Social Fearless

Some people reading this are going to now be thinking that these instructions sound entirely *not* like them. Speak slowly and hold center stage. Gesticulate more and make your motions large. Be passionate and driven…

But what if you are *naturally* shy? What if you freeze up whenever you have to give a talk or even meet someone you don't know very well? How can you overcome natural shyness in order to be the leader you need to be?

One solution is just to start practicing social confidence – and as it happens, this *is* something you can learn. If you keep putting yourself in social situations that you find intimidating, you will eventually start to become desensitized to the stress and you'll stop seeing your heart rate increase and your skin start sweating. You can also combine this with CBT – telling yourself that it really doesn't matter what people think, as long as you are helping to achieve the goal you believe so much in (just one *more* reason why it matters to have passion and vision).

One of the very best ways to face this fear and desensitize? Start doing stand-up comedy classes! You'll very quickly find that you stop feeling anxious when you have to speak with your staff.

Once you do all this and practice building up the level of intimidation, you'll find you stop feeling nervous and it will change the way you come across in public. Now you'll seem calm and collected and people will therefore assume you know what you're talking about and be much happier to follow you!

CHAPTER 5

HOW TO DEAL WITH A CRISIS

This is all good and well – and being able to motivate and inspire your team will get you a long way. But what happens when things go wrong? What happens when it turns out that you don't have enough clients and you're going to have to make cutbacks? This is when things get tough and this is when even your biggest detractors are going to start looking to you for some answers and guidance.

How do you deal with a crisis as a good leader and what is the key to making sure that you come out of any situation relatively unscathed?

Seeing the Unseen

The best way to handle a crisis? That would be to avoid it entirely. Because if you are a truly outstanding leader, then the hope is that you will be able to actually anticipate problems that others don't see and then make sure you avoid them. This is your job as leader – to have one eye on the direction of your business and to be able to look out for obstacles.

This is also why you need to be able to delegate and to set the work that's necessary for your team. This way, they can work *in* the business, while you can work *on* the business. They can keep the machine running while you pilot it.

You can do this by looking at potential futures for your business and thereby seeing what lies ahead. Here are a few techniques you can use to do this…

Planning Fallacy

The planning fallacy refers to the fact that we almost always underestimate how long things take and how much they will cost. When you ask your team 'how quickly can this be done', they will very often tell you '2 weeks' when the reality might well be '3 weeks'. That is simply because we can't account for 'unknown unknowns'. They might not realize that their internet is going to go down for 3 days, or that one of the providers of a key material or tool might take longer than they should to deliver.

So your plan then is to keep this in mind when planning ahead and to insert that buffer so that you can survive even if things *do* take longer than expected.

Scenario Planning

Scenario planning is a form of 'mental simulation'. Essentially, you're going to imagine what you would do in a number of different situations, which is a great way to develop contingency plans while you're not under pressure. Think about all the ways you'd deal with all the things that *could* go wrong – and even imagine your 'doomsday scenario' where everything that can go wrong, does go wrong.

It's also important to keep track of the risks that are currently on the horizon. Keep researching the competition, the markets, trends etc. so that you can find those hidden risks.

Resilience

Resilience refers to a business' ability to withstand hard times. A business can be made more resilient by ensuring it has:

- Low outstanding debt
- Low overheads and fixed costs

- Multiple independent products, even multiple different brands
- Flexible workers and employees
- No 'weak points'
- Fail safes, back-ups and reserves

When things are good, you can work on improving the resilience of your team by improving the efficiency of systems to reduce overheads, by paying off debts, by creating your 'rainy day fund', by accumulating assets or by setting up more revenue streams.

Now when something goes wrong, you should be able to survive for at least a certain amount of time before things turn critical. And when that is the case, your team will see the value in all the hard work you put in during those times of plenty!

Financial Modelling

Financial modelling means creating predictions of your finances based on your current situation. That means looking at your growth curve and how your profits are growing or decreasing over time. It also means inputting the point at which you'll breakeven on any initial costs, looking at overheads and more.

Effectively, this allows you to make projections for your financial fortunes but you can also use these models (which are essentially just graphs and charts) in order to create 'what if scenarios'. What if your rent were to go up 50%? What if a new competitor came on the scene and stole 30% of your sales?

This also means having a good handle on your numbers. This might be work for your accounting team but just make sure that they have done this!

Weathering the Storm

But with the best will in the world, sometimes things *will* go wrong and there won't be an obvious solution.

So now what do you do?

First and foremost, make sure that you *never* point the finger and dole out blame. Doing this is a fast way to make your team resent you and it can also create in-fighting.

Remember: you need to be *responsible* as leader and that means that this is your fault. If it's in actuality Jeff's fault, then it's your fault that you *allowed* it to be Jeff's fault. Jeff should never have been in that position. Jeff is clearly incapable.

49

So you need to take responsibility and that also means taking responsibility in the face of your superiors. This will immediately provide reassurance for your team *and* it will give them confidence in what you say in future. It means your team will know that they can do what you ask and they won't be held accountable if anything goes wrong.

The next thing to do is to *stay calm*. When you panic, it makes the team panic. So be confident and calm and reassure your team that everything will be okay. That doesn't mean lying though – if there is a chance people will lose jobs then you need to let them know that this is a possibility.

What's more though, you should make sure that everyone is working together and on the same page in a bid to get things back on track. Set out a clear course and explain how everyone has their role and everyone should work together. Create a light at the end of the tunnel and a clear plan so that your team can remove their fears by solving the issue.

CHAPTER 6

IS IT BETTER TO BE FEARED OR LIKED?

If you were to stop reading here and just work with all the information we've covered so far, you would now be a leader who was inspiring, courageous and well equipped to motivate their team. You can even help to weather a storm and keep your team motivated and calm when things That's a great start but there's a lot more to it than that.

For example, there is the small matter of knowing how you are going to *control* your team. Because so far we've kind of dealt with an ideal scenario where everyone believes in your vision and you are all working toward the same goal. Like the Queen song…

But what happens when some people *really* don't want to be there? What happens when two people think it's all just a joke?

What happens when someone has a bad attitude and is just trying to create problems for everyone?

This is when leaders can be split into two groups.

You have the one group that will plead with their staff and attempt to be 'liked'. They might make it into a joke, try to be on the 'same page' against the system, or to generally chummy up.

Then you have the other type of leader that will instill fear and tell the member of staff that they will be fired or sent to another department if they continue.

Machiavelli asked whether it is better to be 'feared or loved'. So which is it?

Well, Machiavelli himself actually said it is better to be feared. But that was in a very different time and place.

Suffice to say that it is *not* good to want to be best mates with your staff. This is perfectly demonstrated by the character of David Brent from *The Office* who is more interested in trying to be funny rather than being in charge. Unfortunately, there does need to be some distance between a leader and their team and it's important that you maintain a little respect. Once your team has seen you drunk and curled round a toilet at the office Christmas party, it *will* impact negatively on your ability to instruct them on what to do.

Likewise though, taking a fully 'fear based' approach is also a mistake. This ultimately makes you into the enemy and it creates a stressful work environment for your team. It also prevents your team from attempting to be fully creative or expressing themselves because they will be fearful of repercussions.

So we need to reframe the question. Is it better to be feared or liked? Neither – it's better to be respected. You need to be calm and in charge in such a way that people want *you* to like *them*. That will be a) because they respect you and b) because they understand that you can help them and that you want what is best for the team. If your team sees what you do for them, knows you believe in what you are doing and respects your ability and your capabilities, then they should respect you. If you present yourself as capable, calm and cool, then they should want *your* respect as well.

And guess what? One of the very best ways to gain respect is to show someone else respect. The best way to be *liked* is to be nice to someone to be likeable. The best way to be respected is to be respect*ful* so that there is a mutual understanding.

A good leader needs to be able to work with colleagues from all walks of life and should value what each of them brings to the team equally. In fact, more diverse voices will mean a more diverse set of opinions and views and more diverse skill set!

And so you can occasionally make jokes at your own expense, join in with the fun and even allow others to point fun at you – this shows confidence and strength. The key is to make sure you don't allow this to cross a line and that you don't tolerate staff trying to push their luck by taking a joke too far, seeing how far you will go or being disrespectful. Likewise, you mustn't allow them to test the limits of what they can get away with and this is especially important because it can be unfair on their team and also set a bad precedent. Once one person realizes they can clock off early or stretch their cigarette break to 20 minutes, so can everyone else.

But of course you can't just punch someone who is causing trouble in your team. So what can you do? How can you ultimately demonstrate your authority and get someone to sit down and get on with their work? If your attempts to motivate and to demonstrate the reasons behind your requests aren't working, then what can you do to deal with dissidents? That brings us to the next chapter...

CHAPTER 7

DEALING WITH DISSIDENTS

Of course there is more than one kind of disruption in any team and there is more than one type of problematic member. So the way you deal with insubordination is going to depend on the scenario.

In this chapter we'll look at some options. These will start with the first and most desirable options you have available to you and end with the final and most regretful options.

Transformismo

The first option is to *welcome* the challenge. If someone is not happy with your leadership or the direction you're taking the team, then you could view this as a valid concern. They clearly must have some motivation for not liking the way things are going and that is useful information to you. They have a divergent opinion so instead of staying glued to your confirmation balance – listen to what they have to say and invite them to suggest an alternative option. Often this will take someone so much by surprise that it can earn you instant success.

Better yet, take some one who is trying to encourage more people to side against you and put them in a position of power and responsibility. This is a technique called 'transformismo' that was championed by Italian ruler Mussolini. It's the perfect solution because it a) demonstrates to that person the difficulty of being in your position and shows them that leadership is not so easy as they might like to make out and b) busies them to the point where they can't become problematic.

Or as Sun Tsu put it: keep your enemies close…

Explain and Use Social Influence

Another thing to do is to explain to the person who is behaving inappropriately the damage that they are doing not only to the organization but also themselves and the team. This is once again the power of 'why'.

If someone is going out for longer cigarette breaks for example, then you should simply explain to them that in doing that, they are forcing their colleagues to pick up their slack. If they value their friendship with those colleagues, then they will not like the thought of this and might reconsider their actions. Likewise, you can explain that it has been noted and that when it comes time for a review, it might hold them back for a promotion.

And again, invite them to make a suggestion. Ask them why *they* feel the need to spend outside. Ask them what it is they *want* from this interaction and see if you can come up with an alternative solution. If they feel they can't stand being in the office, then perhaps you need to change the layout of the office? Again, this is a highly effective method as if they feel they're being listened to, then they might feel obligated to give a little as well. Better yet, you might be able to successfully remove the problem altogether.

Of course the temptation here is to make an example of that person and to tell the rest of the team how they're not pulling their weight. This is a mistake because it will a) make that person feel victimized and b) create disharmony in your ranks that will ultimately be bad for business. What you *can* do though is to praise those who are putting in more hours and make sure that they know that you're aware in the difference between their efforts and those of their lackadaisical colleagues.

Carrying Out Punishment

One thing you must *never* do is to shout, get angry or get upset. If you rant and rave at your subordinate, then it will make you appear despotic and it will make the person you are shouting at feel victimized. This can result in people eventually feeling the need to 'stand up to you' and could potentially result in a full scale mutiny.

Moreover, what you're doing here is to completely misunderstand the terms of the agreement between you and your team members (this is a little different for parents).

Ultimately, when you are in charge of someone in a work setting, it only means that they *agreed* to work for your organization. It doesn't mean you have supreme authority of them and you certainly don't have the right to reprimand them as a child. You might be their 'superior' in terms of work hierarchy but you are equal in reality. So what is really going on here is an agreement – the agreement is that they will do what you ask (within reason) in exchange of payment and workplace satisfaction.

If that agreement doesn't work out, then either of you has the right to terminate it at any time. But you do not have the right to make them feel small.

This is why it's highly important *not* to make this permanent and not to make it look as though you have lost your cool. Instead, just keep things polite and civil but carry out what you have to do. And the easiest way to do that? That would be to have a clear set of rules and repercussions for not following those rules. For instance: people caught not working their full set of hours will be required to make up those hours in the evenings and weekends.

With a clearly defined set of actions and outcomes, you can carry out what needs to be done in a cool and collected fashion without making it personal and without it ever seeming 'unfair'. It's the same rule for everyone, they had prior warning and you are simply following a predefined set of instructions.

This is one more reason not to become 'too' chummy with your team though – it can make it hard when you *do* have to take this kind of action and it can lead to accusations of favoritism or personal feelings getting in the way.

CHAPTER 8

CREATING TEAMS AND ENCOURAGING TEAMWORK

One of the best ways to avoid these sorts of scenarios altogether though and to encourage harmony, productivity, creativity and workplace satisfaction is simply to make sure you are putting together the best teams possible and then getting them to work well.

And one way you're going to do this is by hiring the right people…

How to Hire the Right People

Hiring the right person for the job is not simply a matter of picking the person with the best qualifications or experience. Rather, it is a matter of picking the person who will most fit into your workplace culture and who clearly has goals that are aligned with that of the team and the organization. Once again, it comes down to the why and to finding people who really *want* to work there – not only for the money.

If you can do this well, then the people in your office will naturally be friendly because they will have aligned goals. What's more, is that they will naturally be more likely to get on well and to fit into the office 'vibe'.

How to Encourage Teamwork

Encourage Trust

One of the most important ways to build teamwork is to encourage trust. Remember what we said a long time ago about people in the military being willing to sacrifice themselves for their team? The reason that they *all* give for this is 'they would have done it for me'.

You don't have to be best friends with someone on your team and you don't need to share anything in common. But if you can trust them to have your back, then you'll be motivated to support them as well. You can encourage this not with 'trust exercises' (which are a waste of time) but by putting your team in positions where they are forced to rely on each other to succeed. You also need to encourage open communication and openness in general – and you should endeavour to give the team the chance to become personally acquainted so that they know more about one another.

Common Goals

Remember earlier that we said you shouldn't offer individual incentives in order to avoid negative competition within your teams? That still holds true and you should certainly avoid creating an environment where it pays to step on the toes of your colleagues.

But what's more is that you can do the opposite by giving goals for your whole team. Having numbers of sales up on the board, or better yet a customer satisfaction score, can help to remind your team why they're there and to work together toward that common objective. Likewise, giving individual members within the team the credit and autonomy to work on their own aspects, will further help them to be intrinsically motivated and to help their fellow teammates along the way.

Mix Things Up

One thing to avoid is allowing smaller cliques to form within your organization. You don't want one group of 'smokers', the older generation and 'accounting'. While your team will naturally be formed of smaller subsets, cliques can be destructive due to the principles of 'convergence and divergence' which will make those subsets view themselves more like outsiders rather than members of your organization.

Solve this by breaking up destructive relationships by moving the seating and by forcing more interaction between departments.

Understanding

Teamwork between different departments is as important – if not *more* important – than teamwork within departments. This is another reason to move things around and to encourage individuals to spend time in other groups. If someone from sales spends a few days sitting with the marketing team, then they'll not only become less part of their 'sales team boy's club' but will also be more likely to better understand and respect the role of marketing.

CHAPTER 9

UNDERSTANDING CHARACTERS
AND CHOOSING THE RIGHT PERSON
FOR THE JOB

Perhaps the most important part of creating a working team is to understand the importance of different characters and what they can each bring to your organization.

This means firstly respecting and understanding all the different *skills* that your different employees can offer (or your family!). A big part of leadership is delegating and that means you need to know each member of your team well enough to know who is best suited to which job. You can get a workload completed twice as efficiently, simply by giving the right jobs to the right people!

This also means respecting and acknowledging that your team will be better experienced and better equipped than you in some areas. This is important because it is another way you will show respect and give them more autonomy. BUT you should have enough understanding of each of their roles to understand what they're doing and to help offer direction. A good leader in an IT firm should know a *little* about SEO, a *little* about coding and a *little* about marketing so that they can help each member work together.

What's also important though is to understand the differences in personalities, which can also help you to better understand the strengths and weaknesses of each team member *and* help you to better relate to problems they might be having.

Some psychometric tests will define people in a business as falling into one of the four main 'types':

- Dominant
- Expressive
- Introverted
- Relational

The dominant type of course is the 'type A' personality who is loud, driven and high achieving. They might make a good leader someday but they will also undoubtedly rub people up the wrong way until they get some experience under their belt.

The expressive type is the great communicator who is the natural sales person and should thus be given those types of tasks.

Introverts are self-motivated and work well on their own but they *may* be shy (not always) and would probably not be the right people to give presentations or sales tasks to. Conversely, they might be quite creative and useful in those scenarios.

Finally, you have the relational type who is driven by their outward relations and who is a great peace maker and communicator. These people can provide the glue in a team and help to prevent arguments.

What is the best type of personality for your team?

All of them! And if you are going to be making a small splinter cell to send to a tradeshow or to work on a particular project, you'll want to try and include one of each type of person in order to get the most from them all. That way you'll have a lot of different influences, ultimately resulting in the best final outcome.

Of course you can go much deeper than that too with tests like the Myers-Briggs Personality Type Test – but this is a very lengthy and in- depth measure and very time consuming. Ultimately no psychometric test will offer a perfect or complete picture of a person's personality but the key is simply to know your team as well as is possible and to understand how they work with other members of the team and where you can put them to get the most out of them.

CHAPTER 10

THE 10 MOST POWERFUL TIPS FOR LEADERS

So with all that said and done, there is an awful lot to take on board here. Hopefully you have a much better idea now of what really makes a great leader and how you can win the respect of your team and steer them to victory almost without trying.

But still, putting all this into action can be challenging and that's why it's useful to break this down further and to recap on some of the most potent tips we covered throughout the book. So here they are…

1. Have a Vision You Believe In

This is by far the single most important point if you want to make sure your team respects you and that you are making the right decisions for your organization.

2. Focus on Your Mission Statement

As a leader, you need to see the bigger picture and that means focusing on how to deliver results and how to grow the business.

3. Build Resilience and Plan for Contingencies

Make sure that your business is able to handle crises and that you know what you'll do in any of the worst case scenarios.

4. Hire the Right Team

Your team should be diverse in their skills and their abilities but they should be united by the common goal that you all share and the common vision.

5. Give Your Team Autonomy and Credit

This is the best way to make work intrinsically motivating for your team and to ensure they work hard and passionately.

6. Stay Calm, Be Respected

This will keep your team calm and it will make you seem more confident. This is most important when you are challenged by dissidents and when you are going through tough times.

By showing your passion, doing what's best for the team and being friendly but distant, you can endeavour to be respected. This is better than being liked *or* feared.

7. Be One Step Ahead

Use financial modelling and other techniques to stay one step ahead.

8. Take Responsibility

If things go wrong, you must always take responsibility. This gives your team confidence and assurance but also wins their respect.

9. Be Knowledgeable

You won't be the best at anything and you need to know how to delegate. BUT you should also make it your business to understand the role of each team member so that you can oversea the course of your ship.

10. Take Risks

It is important to take risks and be courageous as a leader. This is again what will allow you to grow and what will make your team achieve above the rest.

CONCLUSION

And there you have it. This is everything you need to know in order to start becoming a better leader and to let your authority, passion and wisdom emanate.

And hopefully this is all rather intuitive as you've read through it all. Maybe you've even been able to relate it all back to people you know from your own life. We've all seen *bad* leaders: they're the ones who clearly don't care and who don't want to be there. And they're the ones who want to try and 'act like leaders' by doing the things they think that 'leaders do' – that means micromanaging, making arbitrary rules and shouting at people.

Leadership is none of that. Leadership is something that emerges when one person has passion, vision and a cool level head to execute on their plan to make that vision a reality. If you truly love what you do, people will be inspired to follow you and see what it is you love so much. If you cut a new path through the wilderness, people will be intrigued to see where it leads. And if you have the most knowledge and demonstrate the confidence in how to use it, people will turn to you for advice and guidance. Don't be a leader – just love what you do and be willing to stake everyone on your vision.

Printed by Libri Plureos GmbH in Hamburg, Germany